Poetic Diabetic

Afton Villanueva

Poetic Diabetic © 2022 Afton Villanueva

All rights reserved.

No part of this publication may be reproduced, stored in a retrieval system, or transmitted, in any form or by any means, electronic, mechanical, photocopying, recording or otherwise, without the prior written permission of the presenters.

Afton Villanueva asserts the moral right to be identified as author of this work.

Presentation by *BookLeaf Publishing*

Web: www.bookleafpub.com

E-mail: info@bookleafpub.com

ISBN: 9789395950022

First edition 2022

DEDICATION

To my whole family and to all those who spread pieces of peace

Poetic Diabetic

A Poetic Diabetic
Showing a glimpse into the life of constant checkin and injections
Pouring in drips of dropped blood for inspection
Another test to see if these wings are soaring at the right height or if they need a bit of correction
A diseased lifelong sentence
Could be right
Could be wrong
Depending on your perception
How do you see
The curse disguised as a blessing
Teaching you things that hurt but are designed for protection
Try to recognize its worth
Its worth way more than less than

Prior Diagnosis - Exhausted

Why can't I keep my eyes open
My body and mind's caught in timeless exhaustion
But I'm still tossin and turnin all throughout the night without a precise why
Hopelessly hopin that hopefully
I'll finally find me in a peaceful dream
Maybe if I switch positions?
Toss..
Turn..
Brain sleep!
I keep on wishin..
Turn..
Toss..
Maybe if I lay on top of the sheets?
Toss..
Turn..
Could it be I need the A/C?
Turn..
Toss..
How long has it been since I've had some quality sleep?
Toss..
Turn..
On constant repeat..

Turn..
Toss..
Finally..
I think
I'm beginning to dream..
Then..
Right before it begins..
The clock starts to scream
Once again
Another dark night without sleep
But during the day
I can't stay awake
What is happening to me
Seems like I'm trapped in a dreamless sleep
My brain was so fogged I'd feel lost in my thoughts
Yet my thoughts couldn't even think
Tossin..
Turnin..
Wings burnt
Complete exhaustion

Prior Diagnosis - Dehydrated

Why
Do I
Feel so dry
Why do I still feel so dehydrated after a gallon of liquid's been poured in
Feels like I've been crawling through the desert tryna find another drop that won't stop this unquenchable thirst that's constantly roarin
Inch by inch
Every second
Drip after drip
They never seem to get in
When will I find the divine drip that could get rid of this itchless infection
Caught in a sweltering heat so unique that I'm not even sweatin
Finally find a tiny oasis
Without thinking
I drink it without even breathing
But as soon as I'm done
As soon as the last drop slides past my tongue
It immediately seems like I didn't even taste it
Drank up an island
But this thirst that's inside
It hurts

So I'm still chasin
Waitin
Back on the search
Back to crawling through the desert
Trying to find my divine oasis
I can't help but wonder
Will I ever make it
Will I ever erase this feeling
Of feeling completely dehydrated

Melted Flesh

Bloods turned acidic
Flesh turned to liquid
My eyes
And my mind
Were quickly losin vision
Ignoring intuition
Of guessing what this is or isn't
Even though
The symptoms shown
Gained serious attention
Delirious detected
Foggy thoughts were lost
Still didn't get it
Then
When
I seemed to lose connection
I found myself
Surrounded by help
An early Christmas present

Diagnosed

December twenty first two thousand and nine
An early Christmas present I never expected to find
I was given a gift I didn't even know existed before it was mine
Something that can't be exchanged no matter how hard you tried
A blessing in disguise
There's a couple of types
But your type is the one where you're done if you don't treat it right
Type 1 Diabetic
A present with infinite presence
Connected for the rest of your life
Necessary daily injections
Intended to keep you alive
Don't take too much or too little
The dose needs to be just right
We'll keep you for a week to help find your wings correct height of flight
We'll collect a drop of blood within an electric test strip which will inspect it
Too low or too high
We'll teach you the necessary steps to correct it

Just some of the many phrases said when ol'
Saint Nick gifted this early Christmas present

The Seas You're In

For a couple years after 2009
This thought would cross my mind

When will I realize
I'm not supposed to die
Constantly bleeding
Shot up to eat things
Shoot up right after sleeping
Too low
Too high
My body's bloody roller coaster ride
Who knew this disease would take up
Every action and habit of my life
Why must I just float through
Like a ghost tryin to survive
Until one day
A mistake was made
A choice was chosen
No more needles
No more checkin
I didn't care what it would lead to
No more injections or inspections

A major life selection
Which lead him across the veil

Quicker than expected

A few days or weeks passed
I didn't calculate or bleed
I just decided to eat this or that
No more diet, just sweets and unhealthy snacks
I still remember the orange
That broke the camels back
Creating the ethereal door my withered soul would soar in
Not for a tour
Or to go explorin
But to recieve a message I needed to hear before they sent me back

This pain started deep in my stomach
I knew what it was
But to admit it
I wasnt
There were five black tunnels I fell through
But as far as I could tell
I was still where I jumped through
I wasnt feeling right
And my brother could tell too

Are you alright?

Yeah, I think I just need a drink, or something to eat that's Light

I'll cook up some eggs, and there's waters in the fridge grab what you need to!

I grabbed a drink then sat to think while my brother cooked up a snack to eat
Pain was growin
Unknown?
No, I know it.
When was the last time you took an injection?
When was the last time you bled into a test strip?
Don't you think it's time to grow up and check it?
I guess so.
I need to.
Where was my bag?
Across the room.
Quickly grab and prick your hand to bleed dude.
I got up of the couch.
Almost fell back down.
Weird.
Keep steppin.
You need to check this.
Get to the bag.
Started sweatin.
Unzip it quick.
Fingers slipped.
Don't worry

Just hurry.
Losin my grip.
Grabbed the meter.
Finally.
Sat on my lap.
Time to bleed.
Grabbed the lancet.
But it fell quick and landed next the bag.
Shit.
What is this?
I forgot the word I know I've heard.
This is.
Ketoacidosis.
A complete seizure was takin hold and it won't quit.
I should have listened to the warnings.
Slowly.
Motor skills eroding.
Acidic blood has me messed up.
Can't even sit up straight to check my blood.
Body started shakin.
Felt like the earth was quakin.
But I was the only one swayin.
A forceful learning lesson to always check your blood and take your medication.

My brother noticed, and pulled me to the tub.
Hopefully a cold shower could wake you up.
But.

Before we reached it.
My soul started reachin.
While all feeling in my body was depleting.
My soul kept reaching.
Towards one last tunnel.
But this one.
Was a blinding white light.
Which completely consumed me.
And swallowed me through.
To the other side.
Thoroughly.

The Seas You're Into

Arrived
Blinded
Slowly regaining sight
Soul swallowed whole
By a bright white light
Strangely serene
Curiously calm
I didn't even think
To ask
what's going on
There was no wonder
Of where am I
Or have I died
I just stood
Not feeling bad
Not feeling good
But somewhere in between
Watching the crawling white clouds
Surrounded at my feet
How much time has trickled by
There was no way to tell

Looked up and seen my family
All who passed
Some recently

They each told me
Something profound
They're proud of me and the family
And they're always around
Even if we can't see em
Or hear them make a sound
Then
A best friend whose death was unexpected
Looked at me and said this
Look
I'm not gonna sugarcoat anything
You're fucking up
And you know you're fucking up
And you know what you have to do
You are really here
That's true
But its not the right time for you
You have a purpose
So you're being sent back
Because you need to learn it
Then
The last thing he said to me
Before I returned
Was
Always remember
To take your wings seriously

I came to
Staring at my leg

Which quietly calmed its shake
Returned with a message
Beyond the thin veiled gate

Take Your Wings Seriously

Take your wings seriously
Could really mean anything
Could be your reality
Your creative abilities
Your responsibilities

There's a reason
Why we're still breathin
There's a reason
Why our hearts are still beatin
The sea's you're seein
Could get a little rough
But I ask you please
Just do not give up
We all have a purpose
Don't be nervous
If you haven't learned it
Each and every one of us
Are worth way more than worthless

Breathe

Just
Breathe
Deep
Repeat
Everything will be as it needs to be
If your journey has been full of painful hurting
Know your soul is goin through a thing called learning
Stressful yet bless filled steps will help revive your wings after burning
Breathe
Deep
And see the seeds that have been planted in your hands
Notice the leaves which flow in the breeze
Speakin unspoken words which chose those who truly have heard and believe
Do we understand
That there is a reason why you're still breathin
Follow, Till your leadin.
It may seem like these scenes make no sense at all
But
Could it just be a test to help rise from the fall?

Dia.Won't.Beat.Us

Type 1 Diabetes
No matter how I die
This Dia Won't Beat Us
It'll never leave us
But we won't let it control how you see us
Even though we bleed much
We'll never be bled dry
But
One drip at a time
We'll drop a test strip behind
Like Hansel and Gretel leaving clues for you to find
They'll lead us to belief that our wings will arrive at their correct height of flight
They'll lead us to relief
One bloody drop at a time

A B C's

Another Blood CheCk.
Don't EvEr Forget.
Glucose HIgH?
InsulIn InJectIon.
Ketones: LiL Monsters.
Novolog: Over Pay.
Pancreas: Quit.
RegulaRly & Routinely STabbed.
hopefUlly.
These UncUred Veins Wont cross out my eYeZ.

Test To Correct

Staring past reflections
Thoughts lost without direction
Shifting shadows sifting past those dripping imperfections
Remembered dismembered memories
Caught in locked attention
Study every bloody drop
Electrified inspection
Expect to get an experience with the unexpected
Destined to explain when it contains no explanation
Until you raise the hand to lower with life saving medication you need to inject in

Grippin Drips

This diabetes will not defeat me
As I continue fighting this war discreetly
Grippin with fingertips that are constantly bleeding
I can't lie
Sometimes
It's knocked me to my knees
Weak
Gripping the grim cloak of the ghost that's reaping
Screaming
Stop with the teasing or release me and let me continue breathing!
I shout with a forceful breath pushed from my chest
Silenced the violence
Surrounding all sides
When
A familiar noise started climbin
Heart beating
Vision gettin back its precision as the blood keeps drippin beneath me
Look up to see
A ghastly figure staring back at me
What is this

I asked it
As I felt the sparks within me increasing
You knew this route wouldn't be easy.
Silly Soliloquies as a get back to my feet feeling a little less queasy
I know you will never release me
But know this
As long as this barb wired scarred heart of an organ's still beating, you'll never defeat me
Capisce G??
Then
The scythe held right in front of my eyes lifted releasing its energy depleting grip as it slipped out the door with the wounds of the battle still hittin the floor
Might as well test it
Stumbled to the medical bag and grabbed out the med kit
One more test strip collectin blood to inspect it
Getting back in range
Strange
That was quicker than I expected
One more day
Without my name
Seeing the ink on death's list

inSkullin

In skull! In!
The soul shouted in an exhausted last ditch effort tryna get back in the rotted non-fleshed head it used to live in
A begging demand after the hand forced an injection
A shout which sent crescendoed echoes down the crippled cave of a lifelong sentence
Illusioned views from the lack of light skewed its true perception
Faded, but not erased
Yet
Words never heard
Yet so much more to say
Then
A spark of life caught its eye
A brightly shining type one sign
Maybe this mind is still alive
Another chance to dance
With the hands of time
Come on skull
Let this ol' soul back in
A labored breath to step away from the depths of death
Again

Strange veins contained within the chest began to pulse
There's still more left
An organs formin
A heart rose from rest
Skull to Soul
Hello once again
My long lost wandering friend
Now
Where should we begin

115@634.811

What does this mean?
Does this mean there's more?
One more drop that states there's more breaths I get to take before I reach the gates of heaven and I've got to keep on steppin?
Was guessin until the drip slipped in for testin, a low triple digit creating a piece of peace that we'll comfortably fit in.
I've been saying this for years, through the laughter and the tears, that this is more than just a curse.
I've been blessed in a way that'll save if I can learn from the hurt I've been gettin.
"Its all in your head again my friend."
A soft Whisper that's been swept in.
Not the disease.
Obviously.
But all of the scenes I keep seeing that keep haunting me.
The anxiety inside of me.
Its lying.
Breathe.
Truly see.
Because something worth more than you can believe is closer than you think.

So keep steppin.
Get a quick deep breath in.
Remember,
Its just a curse disguised as a blessin.

270@929.815

Two hundred and seventy at nine thirty in the morning.
Or nine twenty nine
If you want to be precise
Inject to correct with a dose of 2.3 units of insulin
Should temporarily raise the basal rate up to 150 percent.
Hopefully it lowers quickly enough to prevent an amputated limb.
Abruptly, confidence is lost again.
Gain it back, don't lose it my friend.
I keep telling myself but feels as though it was a wet wish I threw down the droughted wishing well.
Wish me well.
It silently shouted as it flipped in spins as it fell down within.
Two hundred and seventy.
Too much of this is gettin to me.
This Glucose has rose with thorns that are embedded in me.
Forcefully sensing its scent which is unfortunately unpleasant to me
Usually

If you choose to breathe in the essence of the rose atop its thorn riddled stem it smells heavenly
But too sweet of fragrance comes with deathly complications
Looks like if I'm going to survive im going to need more medication
Nothing left but to inject
Then comes the fun game of waitin

122@333.825

One One
Two Two's
Three Three's
On the twenty fifth within eight
Someone
Who's true
Will be your destiny
Someone
With new views
Could lead you to pieces of peace
Someone
Will leave clues
To be seen within each scene
Hiding in plain sight
Which one
Will you choose
Once their finally viewed
Wide awake
Or remain blind

One one
Two two's
Three three's
A perfect drip and tick of time to truly test how I could rhyme

To see if I've seen the steps leading to things
divine
Who or what will I see
Will it be
A sign from a diety
Who or what will I find
Who or what will speak to me

139@959.824

Somethin heard the mind
A sign written in time
The gate sent some more
The birds wings could fly
To find within the sky
A place to spend the seconds of its second chance that its been granted after soaring through a skewed view which tore out more feathers than it was used to
How could you mind if you lost it a long time ago
Sounds found inside with profound meanings which are meant with good intentions if you knew how to organize between the truths and lies
Keep progressing with the blessing in disguise
Steep stepping towards the dreams your getting can seem deathfully stressing
Until you finally step from the edge where you're resting
Take your wings seriously as you fly to where you're destined
And always remember
No matter the weather
Never let it sever your feathers connection

To gettin better
And for all the lost feathers
Respect them

Ocean Of Emotions

In this ocean of emotions
Its a miracle this boat is still floatin despite all of the holes that's been poked in
Can feel a real land is still somewhere close
Intuition is whisperin
As I begin to close in
Are you sure there's a shore to show you more than what you're used to?
That's what I'm hopin
Because that's where I'm goin
Riding the seas of seeing
Hopefully reaching
The beaches of believing
With this whole boat riddled with holes
That's still soulfully floatin

Type One Diabetes Mellitus

This
Years
Projections..
Expect

One
Newly
Explained

Daily
Installation
About
Brains
Experiencing
This
Existential
Sickness.

Maybe
Everything'll
Look
Like
Its
Trapped
Under
Sweetness.

Sutillem Setebaid Eno Epyt

Somewhere
Under
This
Imagination
Lies
Little
Explanations
My

Soul
Experienced.
The
Eyes
Blinded
After
Indulging
Directly

Electrified
Noises
Obsessively

Entering
Phosphorescently.
Your
Thoughts?

CPSIA information can be obtained
at www.ICGtesting.com
Printed in the USA
BVHW051010060623
665467BV00018B/1152